Fair Play

Rupak Bhattacharya, M.B.A.

Good Sport

It is important to be a good sport. That means you play fair with your friends.

It means you follow the rules and do not cheat.
It means you are kind when you play sports too.

Jump into Fiction

No "I" in Team

Nick waves his arms up and down.
But Sherry does not pass the ball to Nick.
Sherry never passes the ball to Nick.
That makes Nick sad.

The game is almost over.
Nick waves his arms up
and down again.
Then, Sherry passes the
ball to Nick.
Nick makes the
game-winning shot!

Back to Nonfiction

Teamwork

A good sport remembers to be part of a team.
This might mean passing the ball.
It might mean cheering for other players.
It always means working together.

Easy to Pass

Passing the ball is part of basketball. The players must work with each other to score.

Pass the ball to your teammates.
They will want to pass it to you too!

Manners in Sports

After a tennis match, the players shake hands.
They are saying "good job" in this way.

Teams that work together can score more points.

Scoring helps win games!

Think and Talk

What do these photos show about being a good sport?

Good sports say nice things to their teammates.
They say, "Good job!" when someone tries hard.

Quiet!

Good sports in golf stay quiet when another player has a turn.
But they can cheer for the player after the shot.

Good sports are nice even when things go wrong.
They say, "Great try!" when teammates miss shots.
They help when someone gets hurt.

Good sports are kind to the other team after the game.
They say, "Good game!" when they win and when they lose.

Think and Talk

How are you a good sport when you play?

Fair play is all about great teamwork. Great teamwork leads to great friendships!

Many Places, One Sport

People love to play soccer. They play it in more than 200 countries!

Be Kind

Sherry learned to be a great sport. You can be a great sport too! Be kind to other people. Play fair. You can be a good sport in all areas of life!

VERNON
AMERICAN
ALL STAR
VERNON
AMERICAN
ALL STAR
VERNON
AMERICAN
ALL STAR

Civics in Action

It is not hard to be a good sport. It makes you feel good too. Give this a try.

1. Play a board game with your family or friends.

2. Let someone else go first.

3. Cheer for the winner. If you win, thank the others for playing with you.